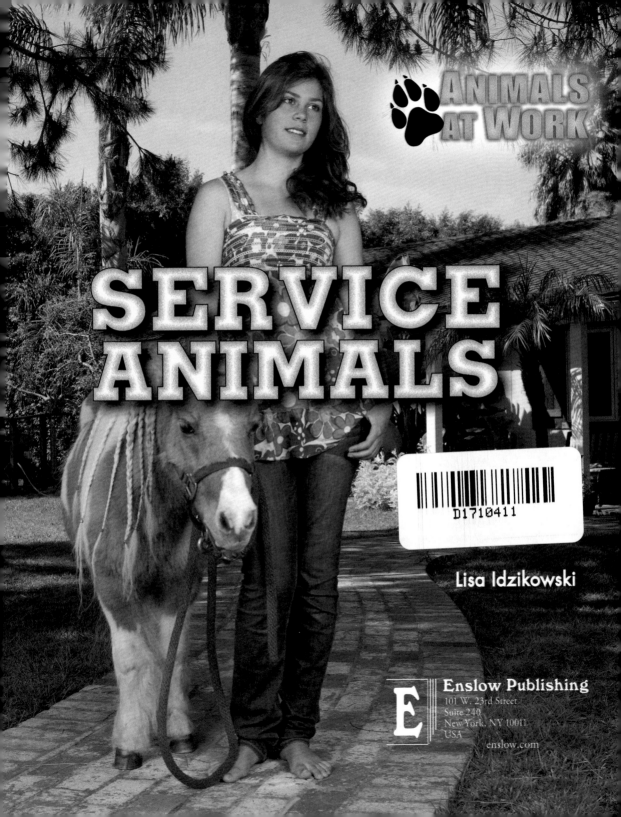

Animals AT WORK

SERVICE ANIMALS

Lisa Idzikowski

E Enslow Publishing
101 W. 23rd Street
Suite 240
New York, NY 10011
USA
enslow.com

D1710411

WORDS TO KNOW

alert To give a sign of danger.

capuchin A type of monkey.

disabilities Conditions that stop people from doing things.

disabled Not being able to do things a person usually can do.

domesticated Controlled and used for work by humans.

handler Owner of a service animal.

mobility The act of moving.

CONTENTS

Words to Know. 2

Chapter 1
Service Animals: Animals Work and Can Help People . . .4

Chapter 2
What Is a Service Animal? 10

Chapter 3
Types of Service Animals 16

Chapter 4
Talk About Work! 19

Chapter 5
Animals in Training 23

Chapter 6
Getting Your Service Animal 27

Learn More 31

Index 32

Service Animals: Animals Work and Can Help People

Animals have lived with people for a long time. As pets, as workers, as friends, and as protection. People are crazy about animals. And many think their animals feel the same about them. People in city apartments love their dogs, cats, birds, and even frogs. People on farms love their animals, too. Goats, cows, chickens, and even llamas. All over the world, people share their lives with animals. And all are better off because of it!

Long ago, people and dogs hunted together. They protected each other. They also became friends. A special bond grew. After a while, other animals became important, too. Goats, sheep, pigs, and cows followed in the footsteps of dogs. Then llamas, camels, and even yaks

A new toy and playtime is the best part of the day!

Nothing beats the feeling of snuggling up to your best friend.

Gobble Gobble

Only about fifteen types of animals have become domesticated. Little by little the process occurred in Asia, Africa, and South America. One of the most recent cases was that of turkeys in North America.

became part of the group. Scientists have ideas how it all began. Sometime long ago, animals and people learned to get along. They learned to help each other. And they found their lives would be better together.

One of these special animals lives in North Carolina. Remington works for a university baseball team. He is a service dog. He came to the university to help the team's trainer. Yes, Remi can carry a ball. Yes, he likes to hang out with the North Carolina players. And he sure is cute. But Remi's main job is to help hurt players. He is their cheerleader. The

Fact
Dogs were the first animals to become domesticated, around fifteen thousand years ago.

Golden retrievers can't resist a game of run and fetch!

young golden retriever can cheer up a player who's in the hospital. He is sweet to someone who is injured and can't play. Players feel good around him. Besides that, he is one smart pup! Remi understands words. He can open and close a refrigerator, turn, and roll over. Remi is one special dog. He is part of a team and an important furry friend!

What Is a
Service Animal?

Go to a mall or restaurant. Walk around an airport or museum. Ride the bus or subway. Places like these are crowded with people. But take a close look. A dog or a horse might be there, too, as a service animal. These animals are not pets. Service animals are smart, highly trained, and doing a job. Some are dressed in work jackets, leashes, collars, or harnesses. Service animals like people a lot. Especially their owners. But when they're out and about—it's all work.

People using service animals are disabled in some way. They need different kinds of help. Some are sick. Some have trouble with mobility. Maybe they are blind. Or they cannot hear well. It could be a child with autism. Or a young person with a certain disease. Suppose

Service animals are always alert when they are working.

Talking Dogs?

Dogs are about as smart as two-year-old children. An average dog can learn 165 words, and really smart ones remember up to 250 words. Border collies, poodles, and German shepherds are the top three smartest breeds of dogs.

someone uses a wheelchair. They'd have trouble reaching a light switch. That's how a service animal could help. A service dog could flip the light on with its nose or paw. Service animals do all sorts of jobs just like that. Hearing dogs are service animals, too. These dogs alert their owners to noises they cannot hear. Perhaps the doorbell rings. Maybe a smoke alarm is buzzing. Hearing dogs let their owners know.

Whoa, was that a horse walking through the mall—wearing a harness and "Reebuck" sneakers? It certainly might have been. Some trained miniature horses are mobility support service animals. They help people who have a hard time moving around. Tonka is one of these friendly horses. His owner needs help with

Some dogs are so smart, they can learn to read.

Some miniature, or mini, horses are pets, and some are service animals.

balance, walking, and climbing stairs. And Tonka is more than happy to help. Disabled people choose guide horses for a few reasons. Some people are afraid of dogs. Some may even be allergic to them. And guide horses live a long time. One thing is for sure, guide horse owners love their animals!

Fact
Service animals are also known as assistance animals, assistance dogs, and service dogs.

Types of Service Animals

Dogs, cats, pigs, and horses. Monkeys, llamas, rabbits, and donkeys. Many of these animals are smart and can be trained. People keep them for friendship. But are they all service animals?

By United States law, there are only two kinds of service animals. The Americans with Disabilities Act, or ADA, says that those are dogs and miniature horses. Because a service animal works by helping its disabled owner do things they cannot accomplish on their own,

Other Types of Service Animals

Some people with disabilities keep ferrets, parrots, pigs, and boa constrictors. Before the current ADA law, these animals were considered to be service animals.

Service animals can travel almost anywhere with their owners — it's the law!

NO PETS ALLOWED WITH EXCEPTION OF SERVICE ANIMALS

these animals have special rights. They can go almost anywhere with their owners. They can ride buses, taxis, and planes. Businesses cannot turn them away. People cannot say the animals must "keep out."

Clever capuchin monkeys are carefully trained to help people with disabilities. But they won't be seen out in public. They are trained to work in and around a person's home.

Rudy is brown and furry. He loves to eat walnuts, peanut butter, and oatmeal. Rudy is a highly trained

Specially trained capuchin monkeys can be a huge help to people in need.

Fact
Monkeys make great service animals because they can skillfully use their hands.

helper monkey. He helps people who have suffered accidents and injuries. Monkeys make smart helpers. They can turn lights on and off. They can open and close doors. And if their owners are thirsty? They can get a water bottle from the fridge, pop in a straw, and bring it over. Now that's talent!

Talk About Work!

Pictures of animals filled prehistoric cave walls. Egyptian tombs made space for animal mummies. Besides being pals, these animals may have helped our long-ago ancestors just like today's service animals.

Service dogs got their start in the United States about forty years ago. Bonnie Bergin saw disabled people in Asia working outside their homes. Donkeys helped them. Bergin knew she had to act. Disabled

Dr. Dog

Some service dogs help people who have diseases, like diabetes or cerebral palsy, that can make life difficult. Others serve people who suffer from seizures or strokes. Children with autism also are helped by service dogs.

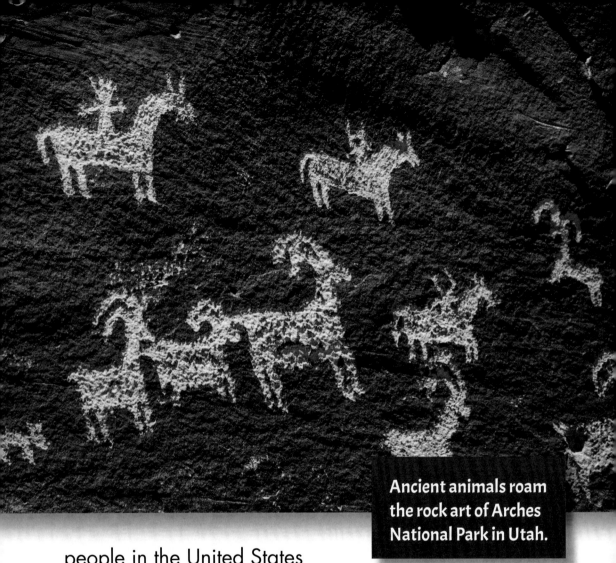

Ancient animals roam the rock art of Arches National Park in Utah.

people in the United States needed help. *Could dogs be the answer*, she wondered? She began training dogs. Her trained dogs helped people with mobility problems. The gentle dogs picked up phones and pens. They opened and closed doors. They turned lights on and off. What a success!

Service animals and
their owners take
breaks and relax, too.

Today, service dogs supply help and hope in many ways. Dogs are super sniffers. They smell so much better than people. Some service dogs are trained to sniff out certain scents on a person's body. They can sense small changes in these smells. These service dogs alert their owners when this happens.

Fact
A diabetic alert dog can smell a high or low blood sugar level more quickly than a machine would notice.

Meet a diabetic alert dog. Diabetes is an illness. It is difficult to live with, especially for children who have it. It can cause a person's blood sugar to be too low or too high. When this happens, that person could get very sick. A Montana family is dealing with this right now. Mom tries to keep her daughter well. But all night long she worries. Will her daughter's sugar level be ok? They are hoping to get a service dog. The dog and girl will sleep next to each other. If the dog senses a change it will give an alert. Sometimes a dog makes a big difference.

Animals in Training

Go to class. Stay focused. Learn. Sounds like a third grader, or a service animal in training. One animal may learn to find the phone. Another may learn to put on music. Others might learn to guide someone across the street. It's challenging work for any animal. But animals are smart. With the right training, they can become service animals.

Service dogs train for about two years. Pups start training when they are eight to ten weeks old. Many move in with puppy-raising families. Pups are taught

Monkey Helpers

There are many different types of monkeys. Capuchin monkeys make the best helpers. They are smart—in the wild they use tools to solve problems and get things done.

Guide dogs are trained to find their way around obstacles.

manners like how to sit, stay, and stop. Their new families take them everywhere and shower them with love. At about one year old pups say good-bye to the family that helped them learn. Then they're off to service school. The playful pups learn more and more. Trainers teach them to focus on their handler. They learn advanced commands like "Get in," "Look at me," and

Horses and their trainers concentrate on the day's lessons.

"Let's go." By the end of training, service dogs are ready for work.

Many young people plan go to college. Helper monkeys go to college, too. They live with families and learn all about people while growing up. At eight to twelve years old, they're off to monkey college. Easy lessons come first, like looking at a person. Soon the monkey learns commands. "Sun," tells this cute helper to scamper over and turn on the light. In five years or less, monkeys are skilled helpers.

Fact
A service dog must be able to do at least three tasks that its handler can't do on their own.

Guide horses train much the same way as guide dogs. They practice moving as fast or slow as their trainer. They also learn how to alert a person to challenges, such as steps or ramps. When it's ready for work, a guide horse will follow more than twenty spoken commands.

Getting Your Service Animal

After a long wait, the day is here. Like wishing for a birthday or holiday, it seemed like the time would never come. Is everything ready for the new service animal?

The service dog knows how to sit, stay, and stop. It is healthy and friendly. It watches a squirrel run across the yard. Or a strange dog on the street. Nothing bothers it. This new service dog keeps focused

Living Long Lives

One interesting reason why some people choose guide horses and monkey helpers is because both types of animals live longer than dogs. Horses and monkeys live about thirty years.

Capuchin monkeys learn all types of tasks at monkey college.

on its handler. It listens. There's one last step. The dog's owner must also go for training. For a few weeks, handlers train with their dogs. They learn how to tell them what to do. They learn how to feed and care for their animal. Together, the new team begins their life.

Guide horses like Cali make it possible for some young people to attend college.

A capuchin has finished monkey college. It can turn on the TV. It can flip the page of a book and scratch an itchy cheek. The last part of training takes place in the animal's new home. A team of trainers spends about a week there. Trainers guide the monkey and new owner as they get to know one another. They teach the monkey helper extra jobs to help with in the home. The trainers also explain what the animal needs in care and feeding. For about a year, monkey college trainers keep close watch and offer any needed help.

Fact
A guide horse or monkey helper could work for much of its handler's life.

Excited guide horse owners know their miniature horse will need extra care. A service dog or helper monkey lives inside the home. But not a guide horse. These animals may spend their days indoors with their owners. They might watch TV or enjoy an afternoon snack together. But when work is done, the horse goes outside. It stays in a large fenced-in yard with a barn. There the horse can relax or run around.

LEARN MORE

Books

Raatma, Lucia. *Animals Helping at Home.* New York, NY: Children's Press, 2015.

Rudolph, Jessica. *Guide Dogs.* New York, NY: Bearport Publishing Company, Inc., 2014.

Rudolph, Jessica. *Service Dogs.* New York, NY: Bearport Publishing Company, Inc., 2014.

Websites

Animal Planet
http://www.animalplanet.com/pets/dogs
Everything you want to learn about dogs, cats, and other pets.

National Geographic Kids
https://kids.nationalgeographic.com/explore/adventure_pass/ amazing-animals/monkey-see-monkey-do
Learn about capuchin helper monkeys.

INDEX

A
Americans with Disabilities
    Act, 16
autism, 10, 19

B
Bergin, Bonnie, 19–20

D
diabetes, 19, 22
disabled people, 10–15,
    16–17, 19–20
disease, 10, 19

dogs, 4, 7–9, 10, 12, 15,
    16, 19–22, 23–26,
    27–28

H
horses, 10, 12–15, 16, 26,
    27, 30

M
monkeys, 16, 17–18, 23,
    26, 27, 28–30

R
Remington, 7–9
Rudy, 17–18

S
smelling, 22

T
Tonka, 12–15
training, 23–26, 27–30

Published in 2019 by Enslow Publishing, LLC.
101 W. 23rd Street, Suite 240, New York, NY 10011

Copyright © 2019 by Enslow Publishing, LLC.

Library of Congress Cataloging-in-Publication Data

Names: Idzikowski, Lisa, author.
Title: Service animals / Lisa Idzikowski.
Description: New York : Enslow Publishing, [2019]
| Series: Animals at work |Includes bibliographical references and index. | Audience: Grades 3-6.
Identifiers: LCCN 2017053156| ISBN 9780766096271 (library bound) | ISBN 9780766096288 (pbk.) | ISBN 9780766096295 (6 pack)
Subjects: LCSH: Animals as aids for people with disabilities—Juvenile literature. | Working animals—Juvenile literature.
Classification: LCC HV1569.6 .I39 2019 | DDC 362.4/0483—dc23
LC record available at https://lccn.loc.gov/2017053156

Printed in the United States of America

To Our Readers: We have done our best to make sure all website addresses in this book were active and appropriate when we went to press. However, the author and the publisher have no control over and assume no liability for the material available on those websites or on any websites they may link to. Any comments or suggestions can be sent by e-mail to customerservice@enslow.com.

Photo Credits: Cover, p. 1 Eri Morita/Photodisc/Getty Images; p. 5 Inti St Clair/Blend Images/Getty Images; p. 6 Unchalee Khun/Shutterstock.com; p. 8 Fuse/Corbis/Getty Images; p. 11 Lawrence Migdale/Science Source/Getty Images; p. 13 Igor Normann/Shutterstock.com; p. 14 Melory/Shutterstock.com; p. 17 JHP Signs/Alamy Stock Photo; p. 18 Micke Sebastien/Paris Match Archive/Getty Images; p. 20 Wade Eakle/Lonely Planet Images/Getty Images; p. 21 iofoto/Shutterstock.com; p. 24 Richard Baker/Corbis Historical/Getty Images; p. 25 Katarina Premfors/arabianEye/Getty Images; p. 28 Melanie Stetson Freeman/Christian Science Monitor/Getty Images; p. 29 AFP/Getty Images.